C000089349

ADVICE FOR A HAPPY LIFE

ADVICE FOR A HAPPY LIFE

Lessons from My Mother

Anne Friedman Glauber

CHANGING LIVES PRESS

Changing Lives Press
50 Public Square #1600
Cleveland, OH 44113
www.changinglivespress.com

**Library of Congress Cataloging-in-Publication Data is available
through the Library of Congress.**

ISBN: 978-0-9849400-7-3

Editor: Lisa Espinoza
Interior design: Gary A. Rosenberg • www.thebookcouple.com
Cover design: Saunak Shah • www.saunakshah.com

Printed in the United States of America

10   9   8   7   6   5   4   3   2   1

Contents

Preface

BEFORE I RELIED ON GOOGLE TO FIND INFORMATION and guidance, my mother sent me clippings. She regularly cut out newspaper, magazine, and newsletter articles, and quotes that punctuated her point of view. When I first got married, at least once a month she would mail two or three clips together in an envelope to me. When I would tear open the envelope, those carefully cut clippings would drop out onto my lap, bits and pieces of advice and wisdom I would then scoop up, put in a desk drawer, and mostly ignore.

A month after my mother died, I went through the desk drawers in her bedroom and found a small stack of envelopes stuffed neatly with her clippings, each one cut perfectly and precisely around the edges, echoing her order and organization by their very form. This time I gathered the clippings close to me. Some were cut from the local papers; some were from the *New York Times* or *Wall Street Journal*. Some were phrases from poetry and short stories; others were from daily advice columns. There were quotes from well-known philosophers, from people who lived in our small Pennsylvania town, from Dear Abby, from her father, from Jewish thinkers and Catholic nuns, and even some Buddhist and Hindu scholars thrown into the mix.

Now, when I read the clippings all together, all in one place, I see my mother's positive spirit and her vibrant approach to life laid out in the pieces of paper before me. It is as if I could hear her voice repeating one of her favorite quotes to me, "The moment is everything. Life is good."

My mother was a success at living. She routinely radiated a sense of purpose and well-being. She always seemed happy—happy in her marriage to my father, happy as a mother, happy in the small town community of north-east Pennsylvania where she lived her whole life. I adored my mother, but I typically challenged her perpetually upbeat personality. I doubted that her happiness could be so real.

My mother never seemed to struggle to find the answers to the many questions I have relentlessly asked myself: *How can I make the most out of my life? How can I be less critical of myself and others? How can I find the core of contentment?* For my mother, those answers appeared to be right in front of her.

And now that my mother is gone, I yearn to understand those answers, too. I miss her positive energy and easy happiness. So, I decided to write about my mother's approach to life. I thought that by describing it, I could keep my mother's spirit alive around me and share that spirit with my children, Lili and David, and with my nieces, my brother's children, Diane and Haley.

And perhaps in the process of writing, I would have a new insight into my mother's distinctive guide to happiness. Because rereading the clippings she cut and kept, some yellow and fragile with age, it is clear to me that these pieces of paper were not just random quotes she liked and saved, they actually framed and contained her approach to living.

Introduction

MY MOTHER LIVED A TYPICAL LIFE IN THE MOST extraordinary way. Happiness revolved around my mother, kept in orbit by her positive energy field.

My mother had a rare sunny character. She felt so comfortable with herself and so at home with who she was that she exuded the feeling that she was always right where she should be. She had the ability to combine a realistic view of life with a continually optimistic outlook that was broadened by her laughter.

When I was a teenager, I would doubt the authenticity of my mother's happiness, and I would rebel against it. I would continually question the value of contentment and look for the creative inspiration found in disappointment and despair. I was interested in the contours of emptiness to counter my mother's fullness.

Still, despite my soul searching, I could not deny the power of my mother's positive personality.

When my mother walked into a room, people moved toward her. It was not just that she looked beautiful—a petite blond with a huge smile and bright blue eyes—but she also radiated a fierce happiness. I saw that people wanted to brush up against that joy and have a chance to touch it, too.

Her positive enthusiasm for even the mundane details of life was surprisingly contagious. Rarely did she become depressed or sad—not even later in life when doctors told her that her chronic leukemia had spread and transformed into something acute.

My mother has been gone for five years now. Her positive energy force is no longer around me. It is only now that I realize that one of the reasons I was able to hold fast to a negative view of the world was that my mother's positive energy field held me up. Now my embrace of the negative is fragile and insecure. Missing my mother moves me to reconsider what I have always dismissively rejected: Is it possible to learn to be positive and happy?

I never thought so. I always believed that people have either the gene for the half empty or the gene for the half full and that's that. And it is practically impossible, extremely difficult and usually a waste of time to do anything about your biological point of view. You're either positive or you are not.

And despite the growth of "positive psychology" as an academic discipline, which I admit to having researched and even enjoyed reading, its practices seem forced and artificial to me. Indeed, there is not one popular positive self-help book on my bookshelf.

But then my mother died. And now I am much more willing to see what I can learn about the way to live a happy positive life.

*"To live in the hearts of those you left behind
is not to die."*

My Mother

MY MOTHER, PAULINE "PAULY" POPLIN FRIEDMAN, lived her entire life in Northeastern Pennsylvania. She was born in Scranton on April 2, 1930, the third daughter of Harry and Lillian Poplin, recent Jewish immigrants from the Ukraine who had met in Scranton. My mother's father, Harry, was outgoing and gregarious, and learned English easily—as well as Italian, because most of his customers were Italian women. Harry had his own traveling sales business, which he ran out of his car, selling every possible item that an Italian housewife in a small Pennsylvania town might need, from curtains and pots and pans to girdles and wedding dresses. My mother was very close to her father, and she was shocked to find, when she was 10 years old, a letter that had arrived not long after she was born from one of Harry's friends, saying, "Tough luck, Harry!"

My mother's mother, Lillian, was shyer than her husband, Harry, and it took a while for her to learn English and acclimate to a new life in the United States. She spent most of her time at home, raising her children. If my mother had difficulties with her mother, who had trouble with reading and writing in English, I never knew.

My mother had two sisters, Florence and Marcella, and the three daughters in the family were all four years apart. Mom grew up sharing both a bed and room with Florence, in a small, three-story house in Scranton. Her father rented out the third floor to tenants for extra income.

It was an easy childhood. Mom shared a similar personality with her father and was popular, funny, and happy. She was a performer and loved acting. When she wanted to give herself a middle name, she chose "Elizabeth" so that her initials could spell "PEP."

It also seemed to be an easy adolescence, with her ability

to laugh at herself. She once relayed a story of how she used to write to soldiers in World War II to give them mail. In each letter, she would tuck a photo of herself and her older sister, Florence. After seeing the picture, the soldiers only wanted then to write to Florence. Mom always had a sense of humor about her sister: Florence was "absolutely gorgeous" and Pauly was "the cute one."

Of the three sisters, Mom was the only one to attend college. Florence became a secretary; Marcella went to art school. My mother first attended Keystone Community College, a small two-year college near Scranton, and then Penn State. While at Keystone, she majored in acting and had all the starring roles in the college's major productions. After two years at Keystone, she attended and graduated from Penn State, where she majored in English and education, planning to become a teacher.

While at Penn State, she was introduced to Sidney Friedman, her future husband, on a blind date set up by her best friend from Scranton. Her friend Sarita had recently married a man from West Pittston, and she introduced her new husband's friend to my mother by saying, "If I have to live in this small town, you have to live here too." Mom listened—and married Sid in 1952, right after her graduation from college. Together, they moved to West Pittston. They were married happily (of course) for 56 years. In 1953, I was born. Eighteen months later, my brother, Robert, was born.

My mother was a homemaker. She raised my brother and me in West Pittston, a coal-mining town that, by the time I was born, had closed its mines. The miners' families now were working in factories across the region. West Pittston was across the river from the town of Pittston, on the shores of the Susquehanna River, whose banks were filled with cherry blossoms in the spring.

Mom and Dad lived in West Pittston for the next 30 years. After living in a small apartment for the first year of their marriage, she and my father built a modern three-bedroom home in a new development behind the football stadium. Dad worked in Pittston in the small electrical supply store on Main Street that was started by his father and where his mother worked as well. He worked seven days a week and every evening, competing with the other electrical supply stores in the region to eventually emerge as one of the largest in northeastern Pennsylvania, with 12 locations.

While we were in elementary school, my mother would occasionally work as a substitute teacher and would refer to her "teaching money" as a symbol of her independence, but she spent most of her time outside of raising my brother and me as an active volunteer and community leader in northeastern Pennsylvania. She was well known in the area as the quintessential volunteer, improving the community with her energy, intelligence, and ideas. Articles about my mother and her work with organizations appeared in the local newspapers almost weekly. Her involvement in the community spanned more than 30 years, and she served and led many organizations in the area. These included organizations that helped families, strengthened health care, supported the local colleges and universities, and improved interfaith relations. She received many honors and awards for volunteer efforts and activism.

In 1984, when my brother and I were no longer living at home, my parents left West Pittston and moved to a home in Kingston, a larger town nearer to Wilkes Barre, in order to be closer to their friends. My mother continued her community involvement and leadership.

When my father was in his mid 60s, he started to work

less. He and my mother took up tennis and golf, had a very active social life, and bought an apartment in Florida, where they would stay for several months every winter.

In 1998, my mother was told that she had chronic lymphocytic leukemia (CLL), a slow-growing leukemia that could go untreated for several years. She had lived with the disease, which grew progressively worse, for ten years when it transformed into lymphoma. Throughout, she kept up a busy schedule, an active social life, and maintained her community involvement and leadership until the last two years of her life.

She died December 17, 2008.

A Philosophy of
Living a Happy Life

AFTER READING THROUGH THE DOZENS OF CLIPS AND articles my mother collected, I organized a top-nine list that encapsulates my mother's approach to living a positive, happy life. She melded the practical with the ideal, balanced the seriousness with the absurd. She gave, but with boundaries. She connected with people, but thought independently. She maintained a powerful positive outlook, coupled with a shrewd assessment of reality. It was the mix that mattered.

And perhaps most important—and what I want my children, Lili and David, to know as they build their lives— is that my mother continually shaped how she saw her life. She was in charge.

My Mother's
Top 9 Lessons

1. Be disciplined about the positive—and practice it.

2. Be in the present—and use it to move forward.

3. Be a listener—and limit what you say about yourself.

4. Be at your best at all times—and don't be a perfectionist.

5. Be proud of your religion—and respect all religions.

6. Be funny—and do not laugh at jokes that undermine you.

7. Be connected to nature—and stay connected.

8. Be a giver—and set limits.

9. Be involved in something larger than yourself—and stay involved.

1. Be disciplined about the positive—and practice it

ॐ

"The secret of staying young is keeping a positive self-image. Futility, pessimism, frustration, and living in the past not only are characteristics of old people but also are the very characteristics that have made them old."

Mom's advice about being positive

- Reinforce it.

- Direct it to yourself.

- Let go of anger.

- Forgive.

- Find gratitude.

When Mom wanted to make a point about attitude, she would tell me the story about her father and the dentist.

She would proudly say to me that whenever her father went to the dentist to get his cavity filled, he would never use any Novocain. He would refuse to have the injection and then proceed to get his cavity filled without any relief from the pain. This would confuse me. I could not figure out why my mother would be so proud of that fact. Why would anyone voluntarily endure pain if he had any choice?

My mother would then tell me that the reason her father did not use Novocain was that he knew that he would not need it. He understood how the brain and the body were linked. "He thought his way through the pain," she told me. "You can, too."

She consistently repeated her father's words to me, even as a child, saying, "Always remember this: You are in charge of yourself." As I child, I did not realize how challenging a premise that could be or how many choices would emerge that would complicate that basic statement. But for my mother, it was simple. "Be in charge of your attitude and you are in charge of yourself."

This was my mother's essential wisdom. She believed that it was possible to control how she saw her life, and she chose what was most natural to her. She chose the positive. But what I never realized until I saw all the many quotes she had saved was that being positive was a discipline. She continually sharpened her positive point of view. When so much of life was beyond control, what gave my mother a sense of certainty was her attitude.

"Attitude is its own discipline."

What I have come to see is that throughout my mother's life, her positive discipline trained her to feel the tranquility in a day that could be filled with anxiety. That was what she meant about her father and the Novocain.

"Write it on your heart that every day is the best day in the year."

Reinforce it.

My mother always seemed happy, not complacent or passive—but profoundly happy every single day. That's an extreme statement I know, but the odd thing is that her happiness was absolutely ordinary. It was not some false sweetness or a refusal to face a disappointing reality; it just shaped how she encountered the events of her day. Of course she would have times when she was tense or annoyed, but her happiness came from a remarkable ability to make her positive attitude supersede anything else.

When I would ask her, "What point in your life were you the happiest?" she would look at me and answer not in a syrupy way at all, "Wherever I was, I was the happiest."

That answer left me speechless. "Really?" I would counter. "You were never miserable?"

She would simply say, "No, not at all. At each stage of my life—and life is about stages—I was happy."

The reality was, her life as a young housewife and mother was a routine of sameness even though that routine focused on my brother and me. My father came home every night for dinner exactly at 5:00 p.m. in order to be back at work in his store at 6:00. No matter where we were or what we were doing, we had to be at the dinner table at 5:00. Mom cooked dinner practically every weekday night. When we were young children, we rarely ate out as a family, with the exception of occasional restaurant visits for barbecue sandwiches on Sunday nights.

Dad ate dinner quickly because he was going to go back to work. After dinner, my brother and I would sit around the table with my mother and talk. If she was upset that Dad ate so quickly and left, we never knew. Mom had us laughing and talking. If Dad was stressed about his work or was quiet at dinner, Mom would not take it personally or seriously. She would just say, "Don't mind Dad's moods. If he is grouchy, it is just that there is a full moon." And she would laugh. I would then open the door to peek outside to check up on the moon, and there it would be, full and reassuring.

Dad worked seven days a week. He was gone many evenings as well. We practically never went on vacations together as a family. I remember only once going away for a long weekend in Atlantic City, with my father joining us for the last day and a half.

Mom was basically a sole parent, attending by herself sporting events for my brother and school events with me, handling car pools, homework, and music lessons—

everything. We grew up in the 1950s and that was the pattern. I never heard her say, "I wish Dad were around to help." Mom would say how lucky she was to be the major parenting influence. She would tell us that she was pleased she did not have to argue about discipline, rules, or parenting choices with my father; she was the decision maker. Someone else may have complained about being on her own so much, but Mom focused on the positive aspects of raising her children alone without any interference.

Mom's mentor in the positive was her father, Harry, the man who needed no Novocain, whose six grandchildren all called him "Bobby." When Bobby was losing his eyesight in his late eighties, Mom would repeatedly tell us how he would never complain and would instead see the humor. He would go out for a walk with her and, as he bumped into something, he would make fun of his own dimming eyesight saying, "Excuse me, Mr. Bush," "Mr. Tree," or "Mister Curb."

Even if you're blind, my mother was saying to me, you can work hard to envision a better reality. It's up to you. You are in charge of what you see. Focus on seeing the positive.

"Who is a rich man?
One who is content with his life."

Her father's favorite quote was from the Pirkei Avot, "Lessons from Our Fathers." Even though my mother did not know Hebrew, she kept the quote both in Hebrew and in English in her clippings and would repeat it to me in both languages many, many times. She put it on the tombstone of her father's grave.

Because contentment was not what I was aspiring to when I was younger, because struggling and yearning were more intellectually appealing, I would discount the statement as an easy excuse for not seeking deeper answers. Now as a middle-aged adult, I know how extremely elusive that quality of contentment is.

My brother frequently tells the story that he would call my mother every morning when he was driving to work. During the course of these thirty years, every day, he would ask that general question, "How are you?"

No matter what, instead of saying, "Ok," "Not bad," or "Alright," my mother would always answer my brother by saying in an upbeat voice, "Wonderful! I am wonderful today." Her response never changed—and every time, the two of them would validate the consistency of her answer with their laughter.

My mother's statement now fills me with wonder. If I said that I was wonderful every day when my children called me, would it make it so? If I told myself and others each morning how wonderful I felt, would it shape the way my day would unfold? My week? My life?

> *"Healthy people think well of themselves. They don't waste time and energy worrying if every hair is in place or whether they have made a good impression. They have a good sense of priorities and a sense of what is really important."*

> *"This above all: to thine own self be true."*

Direct the positive to yourself.

My mother often would tell us how important it was to simply love yourself. "If you think well of yourself," she would say, "you will think well of life." To reinforce that point, she would add, "You have to love yourself first before anyone else can love you."

That was always a difficult piece of advice for me to hear because I had a habit of criticizing myself frequently. That made no sense to my mother. She did not think that intense scrutiny was very effective.

Still, Mom was not without remorse for her own mistakes. From time to time, she would tell me about a disagreement she had had with a friend or a disagreement she had had with her parents, but she would rarely dwell on these events or spend time analyzing and reanalyzing. Directing the positive lens to herself gave her energy to move on and not linger over mistakes.

"Don't let other people define you."

Let go of anger.

If people were angry at my mother or had problems with her, she would recognize it, apologize, and move on. In turn, if she was angry about something, she would express it and then let it go, so it would not deflate her positive energy.

"Don't let anger eat you!"

My mother would tell me frequently that holding anger toward someone was more hurtful to me than to the other person. She exemplified this in her own actions. When she fought with my father, I rarely remember a time when she sustained her anger for more than a few hours. She was all for "blowing off steam," as she phrased it, expressing how she felt and then letting the anger fade away.

Throughout her life, as her interests changed, she had many friends come and go, but it never seemed to me that her friendships ended out of any anger, as she never appeared to harbor expressed or unexpressed grievances. It was not worth it to her to hold on to anger. In fact, she thought it was dangerous to health and happiness. Stewing in anger cooked up a negativity that could permeate everything else.

"Forgiveness is an opening to ourselves."

Forgiveness was the natural complement of letting go of anger. My mother felt it contained fuel for the positive. I had a lot of anger during and after my divorce for many years; it choked me and filled me with resentment. Although it created a disturbing level of stress and anxiety for my children, I could not see past the anger. It would rise up especially during periods when I was trying to have a working relationship with my ex-husband.

But during those times, Mom would have considerable patience and empathy for my ex-husband, constantly urging me to make peace and reach out to him in friend-ship. That attitude confounded and annoyed me. I felt that somehow she was negotiating with the enemy and urging me to do so as well.

Constantly, she would say to me, "Anger will hurt you; just move on."

One Rosh Hashanah (the Jewish New Year), many years after our divorce, during a time of ugly recriminations around some issue, Mom made certain that she set aside a portion of her brisket—which my ex-husband loved—and made sure that I gave it to him. I was frustrated with my mother for saving her brisket for him and wondered why I was rewarding bad behavior with a gift.

But despite my annoyance at both of them, I gave him the brisket—and even added in an extra amount of gravy. The meat mediation proved effective. It created an opening between us that eased the tension, teaching me the power of letting go of anger (and a good brisket).

The force of forgiveness penetrated another difficult time. During the last few years of my mother's battle with CLL, we were so concerned about the course of the disease that my brother and I asked her to consider switching doctors. She relunctantly made the switch, but in a small town that was not easy. Her prior doctor was not happy, and in a formal letter he wrote her, "not to come back to his practice again."

During Yom Kippur (the Day of Atonement), three years before she died, my mother saw that doctor at synagogue and made a point of speaking with him. She walked directly over to him and said, "If I hurt you in any way, I am so sorry. Please forgive me."

Mom told me that as she talked to him, she started to cry. The doctor was startled and surprised and told her that all was okay. "She need not worry," he said. When her other doctor left town unexpectedly, and she needed to go back to her original doctor, he was there to treat her. It showed me how powerful the expression of forgiveness is.

Find gratitude.

"Healthy people are able to accept whatever life visits upon them without going to pieces. This means financial reverses, illness, death, divorce, separation, unrequited love—the list is endless. And they have the ability to withstand the cruelties and inequities of life, to regroup, re-energize, and go forward in a positive and constructive way."

My mother could accept what could not be changed through gratitude.

I was with my mother when her oncologist first told her that her leukemia had transformed into something worse. We were at Memorial Sloan-Kettering Cancer Center in New York. The doctor told my mother that her disease had progressed to a new life-threatening condition. I looked at my mother's face and saw her swallow hard. Something briefly passed through her eyes and then her focus shifted. She did not express fear or question the severity of the diagnosis. I saw her immediately go into a positive constructive mode. She asked, "What's next? What treatment do I need? I just want to get it over with so I can focus on life."

The doctor explained the treatment choices. My father, mother, and I discussed the options, and the two of them then got into the car and returned to Pennsylvania to begin the treatments. It wasn't that she gave up. She kept on fighting for her health, seeing doctors, and exploring new approaches. It is just that she absolutely refused to allow that diagnosis to impact her love of life.

By not focusing on the illness, by not making it the centerpiece of her existence, she was able to just live. It made it easier on us as well.

Throughout her illness, she did not complain. All we heard was gratitude for living. "I have had such a wonderful life," she kept on saying.

"Keep my tongue free from endless details.
Seal my lips on my aches and pains."

During the last year of my mother's life, as she became increasingly weak, she could hardly leave the house. I asked her if she ever got bored, and Mom would reply almost fiercely: "Never!" She would continue, "This is life. What could be boring about life?"

The last Thanksgiving with Mom, she said she wanted to make the first toast before our meal. It had been a difficult autumn. Mom had been in the hospital, much weakened, in pain, and had only recently barely overcome a severe setback that made it difficult to walk and get around. But none of that was reflected in the toast she gave to us that Thanksgiving. What she said was, " I am so lucky." She went on to describe her great luck, naming those blessings in great detail and offering them up to us as the centerpiece of the day.

Looking back on that Thanksgiving, I realize that by giving that toast to us, my mother was simply practicing her discipline. Just as a true master practices any talent, my mother practiced the positive every day, showing us its value in the happiness she created around us.

2. Be in the present— and use it to move forward

ॐ

"Bacarim, bacarim, chadashim. . . ." (Hebrew)
"Every morning there is something different."

Mom's advice on living in the present:

- Focus on the present.

- Use the present to plan.

- Take risks.

- Keep sentimentality at a distance.

- Be present even in difficulty.

My mother's father, "Bobby," taught her to live in the present. He taught her from a young age, with simple lessons that left lifelong impressions.

"We would gather around the dinner table for dessert," my mother would say. "All of the three daughters would wait as he set peaches on the table to eat. We would reach for the peaches, and my father would stop us. 'Wait,' he would say. 'Let's really taste a peach.' "

"The moment is everything. Life is good."

He would then take a knife and slowly cut little slices from the peach and give pieces to everyone—my grandmother, my aunts, and my mother. As the summer juices ran down the pieces, he would say, "Eat it slowly, smell it, see it, and taste the peach."

Mom said that what she learned is that we can't be in a rush all the time; we have to take the time to really taste.

"She she yeah jess, dalshe boojess" (Russian)
Translation: "The slower you go,
the further you will be."

Mom was trained by her father to savor each day. So many of the quotes that she saved stressed the importance of paying attention to the present, commenting on it, and identifying what to praise in a day. Laughing, talking to us, connecting to nature—I felt like she gave her complete attention to what and who was around her, and it sensitized her to the fullness of life.

It was an element that came through in her cooking, too. As she cooked, she paid attention to the ingredients and to the fragrance of fresh vegetables and herbs. I remember her making even a simple breakfast with full concentration of the moment. To season the breakfast, she would go out to the backyard to her clay pots, which were filled with herbs, chives, parsley, and dill. She would smell them, admire them, chop them up finely, and whip them into her scrambled eggs, which tasted so fresh and special, like the morning.

"Yesterday is a memory. Tomorrow is a mystery. Today is a gift. That is why it is called the present."

Concentrating fully on the present expanded my mother's capacity for joy. It was also a way to counter regret. My mother used the present to move forward.

She told me this story often, especially when I was upset about something.

She said, "Just a few weeks after graduating from Penn State, where I lived in a sorority with dozens of friends around me, I married your father. We moved to the small town of West Pittston, where your father was working 12 hours every day at the store."

Mom then proceeded to tell me that they found a second-floor apartment in a two-family house where they lived on a tiny, dead-end street on the west side of West Pittston.

"Your father worked nearly all the time," she said. "He would come home late, work weekends, work nights, and I was left alone." She was lonely, adjusting to her first year of marriage, wondering what she had gotten herself into by marrying so soon after college, and moving to a small town where she knew only one other person.

Then one evening, she had had enough. "I was so upset and frustrated," she told me. "I had an argument with your father about spending more time with me. I left the apartment and walked three blocks to Dressler's Pharmacy to use the pay phone to call my mother." She said to her mother, "I don't want to be alone like this."

Her mother, my grandmother Lillian, replied, "Is your husband out gambling? Is he running around? Why are you complaining? He is working hard to build a secure life for you and your family. Go home and appreciate him."

My mother listened to her mother, turned around, and went home.

She told me the story countless times at many points in my life. She told me the story when I first got married and moved to New York City and lived above a Greek coffee shop in the East Village when my husband was in law school, and we had little money. My mother told me the story when I moved to New Rochelle and had a year-old baby, a large house, and a husband who had some difficulties adjusting. And she told me the story—many times in fact—when I moved back to Pennsylvania after living in New York for 23 years.

Each time she would tell it, it was like it was the first time. Even when I chimed in and told her what my grandmother said at that critical point in the story, Mom would just go on, ignoring what I said and continue the story and its ending as if I had never heard it before.

Telling and retelling that story was a seminal insight for my mother; Don't weigh the past against the present. Live where you are and go forward.

"Think only of the past as its remembrance
gives you pleasure."

"Bloom where you are planted."

I made a decision to move back to Pennsylvania from New York after my brother suggested that I join the family business, where he had been working since college. Although my career and life had been in New York for two decades, the idea seemed appealing. After being a single mother for six years, I was finding it much more of a struggle. I had the sole responsibility for my children and a demanding work schedule. Moving back was moving to an idealized simpler life, back in my hometown.

However, things were not as I expected. The new job in electrical supplies had little connection to my twenty years of work experience in the field of international public relations. With a home in the middle of the country and no friendly neighbors, and my son angry at being moved from New York, it was hard to appreciate the present. I expected a simpler life, but what I got was paralyzing regret.

I was filled with nostalgia. Although I had been unhappy in New York, the past now seemed positive and the present filled with problems. I realized that I had a strange way of dealing with my world: the present was negative but as soon it became the past, it was wistfully positive. I found the positive in the past and the negative in the present, shifting my way through regret and despair.

Mom had little interest in nostalgia and even less interest in thinking of what could have been. That was her point: Concentrate on the present and look to improve it.

This did not mean she advocated passive acceptance. On the contrary, focusing intensely on the present provided her with a clear sense of how to analyze the facts and plan well for the future. We often discussed what the next steps would be after my son graduated high school and I returned to New York. When I wanted to keep the house in Pennsylvania for a while so Dave could have a bridge to his past after he graduated college, she said, "Sell it as soon as you can and move on."

*"For me the driving force since the beginning
has always been good work, taking risks,
trying new things. If the door opens,
go through it. Always go forward."*

Being fully in the present helped her to think through ways to successfully move onward. She concentrated on what the actual situation was—not her expectations or wishes for what it could be. It enabled a confidence in taking risks.

"Our lives improve only when we take chances."

My father often tells me the story of how my mother's view of risk had a pivotal impact on his business strategy. My father was in business with his father for many years, before my grandfather retired. During the course of their partnership, my grandfather would dissuade my father from buying new stores to expand the business.

Then came Mom. When he debated about whether to buy another store, and he shared with her his worries about the costs, payments, and responsibilities, Mom did not hesitate. After hearing his concerns and fully recognizing the risks, her response was simple: "Go for it." It was a decision he never regretted. The new business was a success, giving him the foundation to continue to expand his business considerably in the next twenty years.

"Change is a good thing."

My mother's connection to the present generated an approach that was somewhat counterintuitive. While she had the most remarkable ability to live in the present, she also firmly believed that changing the present could be very beneficial. Getting stuck in a rut could numb you. Taking risks, following up on a dream, and changing the current reality to solve a problem and shake up the present were all strategies my mother advocated.

Mom's risk-taking style was not just about expanding a business. It was also about attitude.

"Taking risks gives me energy."

What always was both laughable and astonishing was that my mother would never hesitate in approaching a well-known public personality for the events she would organize for her many nonprofit causes. She would find a direct phone number somehow and persist until the person would agree to speak at one of her programs. She was never intimidated by fame or celebrity.

She would chair the annual meeting for the Family Service Association, for example, and happen to read about a best-selling book about family dynamics and then figure out a way to reach the author and national expert. The next thing I knew, that person would be speaking at the Family Service Association meeting in Wilkes Barre, wondering I am sure, how she ended up there. Mom managed through the years to get every one of my interesting PR clients to come to Wilkes Barre—from the CEO of Ford Credit to the head the of the Journalism School of Belgrade, Serbia. No one could refuse her. As she often said, "What do I have to lose? The worst thing that can happen is that the person will say no."

*"Look to this day. For it is life,
the very life of life."*

*"In its brief course lie all the verities and realities
of your existence: the bliss of growth, the glory of
action, and the splendor of achievement. For*

yesterday is but a dream. And tomorrow is only a vision. But today, truly well lived, makes every yesterday a dream of happiness and tomorrow a vision of hope. Look well, therefore to this day. Such is the salutation to the dawn."

About a month after my mother died, I went back to my parents' house and went through my mother's closets with her housekeeper, Colleen. We were sorting the clothes, figuring out what to do with them—what I would take, what would go to others, what would go to the Salvation Army. It was difficult to do it so soon after my mother's death, but a friend had said to me that if I didn't part with my mother's clothes quickly, I might want to keep them forever and never let them go.

Although it was a very private and difficult thing to do, I was relieved to do it with Colleen; it was too painful to do alone. Together, Colleen and I silently and slowly went through my mother's walk-in closet, with its orderly stacked sweaters, jackets, and shirts. As we emptied it and put clothes into piles, Colleen turned to me and said, "I always saw your mother happy. Even when your mother got weak, when it was tough to walk or even sit, your mother always seemed to be so happy."

Happy. Colleen's words brought me back to my own words. So often in my life, especially during transitions, my mother would tell me to "bloom where I was planted" or that "each day was special." I would grit my teeth and tell her in a condescending way that it was easy for her to say "be happy," because her days were easy, stress-free, and financially secure. I would tell her that her advice had little resonance because our lives were so different. I was a single mom, raising my children, managing a demanding job, figuring out an uncertain future.

But that day in my mother's now silent bedroom, with the shades drawn and shutting out the faint January morning light, I realized that the source of her advice did not come from an easy life; it was far deeper than that. When she became sick and fragile, when her life was more constrained and limited, she did not vary. She continued to do what she did so well, and what she continued to urge for me, "Look to this day—for it is life, the very life of life."

It was the source of happiness and strength.

3. Be a listener—and limit what you say about yourself

Mom's advice on the value of listening:

- Listen so you can see.

- Ask good questions.

- Trust a few.

"If anybody asked me to describe my greatest asset, I would say, I am a connector. I just have an instinct about who needs to know whom and how to connect to people and ideas."

The day of my mother's funeral, after returning from the cemetery in the midst of a raging snowstorm, we gathered for a sit-down luncheon at an event space in a hotel where my wedding reception had been held thirty-two years earlier.

During the lunch, I sat with my father and brother at one of the ten round tables covered with a pink table cloth, listening to people stand up by their tables to toast my mother and talk about how they knew her. It was hard to concentrate and listen. Instead, what I heard was my mother's laughter, three months before.

"I would like a lunch after the cemetery," she had said.

Mom was very weak then and spent a good part of her day lying in bed, creating a sort of office there with her papers, calendar, and notes of to-do's she always had by her side near the pillows. Her request caught me off guard. "What do you mean?" I asked.

She laughed and said, "I want to make sure that we have at least several hours for everyone to give their speeches about me. We will need a lunch to do that."

So together, we started to plan it, like we had done for all of her parties, discussing a guest list (do we include that friend or not?), reviewing the menu (cold dishes or hot?), deciding about drinks (shall we serve liquor?), and thinking about ambience (do we want music, and if so, what kind: mournful or celebratory?).

All the time that we were planning the lunch, we were laughing at the absurdity of planning and laughing to stave off our fear. We laughed as we described how we would set the tables in the room and the food everyone would eat, we laughed as we described how the speeches would proceed and who would be the master of ceremonies, and as we laughed, we clasped hands together to hold the laughter in front of us like a flimsy barrier against a raging storm.

Three months later I now sat silently at the funeral luncheon listening to the eulogies of her friends. A new friend of my mother stood up to tell her story. She spoke softly as she told us, "I am a member of Friends of Family Service. When I joined the organization two years ago and introduced myself, the president of the board asked all twenty-five people at the meeting to share how they got involved with the organization.

"As we went around the table, every person there looked at each other, and just said, 'Pauly. Pauly asked me to become a member, and I could not refuse her.'"

My mother had a sizable talent, which she used frequently and successfully to connect people to her organizations and to each other. When my mother would first meet someone, even in the most casual of circumstances, eventually somewhere in the conversation she would suggest that the individual join one of her nonprofit boards. Inexplicably, that person would say yes, and that connection would last for decades. I cannot remember anyone saying no to my mother. Somehow in her ability to truly listen to people, she could understand intuitively what would fulfill them.

Mom was a "connector," so when I was asked to take on an interesting public relations assignment for the U.S. Agency for International Development to help publicize the first nonprofit foundation for a hospital in Warsaw, I recommended her to the project director as a consultant.

She was an ideal candidate because the project needed individuals who had first-hand knowledge of how to gather community support for a nonprofit cause. I could not think of a better advisor than my mother, who had served on nearly every major board in the Wilkes Barre community and knew how to sell a cause.

So, in less than twenty-four hours, Mom, who had never had a job outside of a few substitute teaching assignments, created 1,000 business cards that read, "Pauly Friedman, Consultant to U.S. AID." Two weeks later she took off from Kennedy Airport as an official member of the U.S. AID project delegation on a mission to Warsaw. The project director started each day at breakfast at 7 a.m., and kept everyone to a strict agenda of at least six major meetings a day. My mother was there for a week, meeting with potential board members, funders, and volunteers in the Polish community. She was especially fond of the newly appointed head of the first foundation, Dr. Adam Jelonick, a medical doctor who became its director.

In the course of one week, she got to know his life story, details about his family, his concerns about his new job, and his plans for the future. Importantly, she helped him shape a legacy of philanthropy in Poland. She was one of nearly ten consultants who advised the first nonprofit board of a hospital foundation in post-Soviet Warsaw, and she was one of a few who had a lasting impact. She connected this nascent board in Poland to all she knew in Pennsylvania and beyond.

When Mom returned to her home, she called a meeting of the influential Polish residents of Wilkes Barre—the heart surgeon, the lawyer, the banker, the community leader. She briefed the local children's rehabilitation institute on her mission, and through her persuasiveness and her own fundraising, ensured that Adam Jelonik made a trip to Wilkes Barre to meet all these potential supporters.

To help build their support, she hosted a dinner party, inviting everyone—from the local congressman to the mayor to the presidents of all the major hospitals and universities—to meet Adam and hear firsthand how they all were going to support the foundation for the hospital. No one could resist my mother's sheer joy of connecting people and making things happen.

After fifteen years, this connection still exists. The Wilkes Barre community is still supporting Litefska Children's Hospital, with extraordinary donations of medical equipment and ongoing funding. Art exhibits from the children at Litefska Hospital come to Wilkes Barre every year, and many of the people whom Mom invited to the party are still making funding trips to Warsaw to support the foundation. And, through her support for Adam Jelonick, his daughter made her way to the Wilkes Barre area and married a man she met there.

"Please give me the ability to see good in unlikely places and talents in unexpected people. And give me the grace to tell them so, dear Lord."

Mom connected people to her organizations; she also had a way to help them connect to their true selves. It is difficult to describe what powered my mother's ability to detect people's talents. I believe it was how she listened. She listened and saw beyond what a person looked like, where they came from, or what they wore.

Once she identified a talent, often one that may have been unnoticed even by the person herself, Mom would then promote this talent to anyone who would listen. Mom would continually praise the talents she found in the people around her. She would call me to tell me about her gardener and describe in great detail his ability to trim and shape her bushes with the skills of a sculptor. She would not only tell me; she would tell the gardener himself. She would praise his skills and reinforce his self-esteem, helping him to see himself in new ways.

When Mom was on the board of the local Penn State campus and engaged in their capital campaign, she became very friendly with the successful and charismatic president of the campus and his beautiful wife. She would tell people how impressed she was with his administrative talents. She was a key advocate, and many people felt the same way in the community.

She also praised and promoted the development director at the time. The development director was quiet, thoughtful, and shy. Yet, my mother heard her intelligence and appreciated her competency and made sure others recognized it as well. In fact, Mom recommended that this woman join a subsequent mission to help the Litefksa Children's Hospital in Poland, and this experience changed her view of what was possible.

This ability to truly listen to someone forged so many connections for my mother. These connections not only fulfilled my mother's life, they impacted so many others. During my mother's funeral, I heard so many people say to me, "I felt like I was the most special person in your mother's life. She seemed always to hear me."

One person after another would tell me stories about how my mother heard them. "Your mother found out that I wanted to open an art gallery," "go back to school," "start a business," "be a painter," "become a teacher," they told me. She encouraged them and supported them in their dreams. She would talk to them, help them plan a strategy, connect them to people who could help them, and then promote them to her friends. Mom had an ability to hear a person's quiet aspiration—and if she thought it was possible, she would figure out within her networks how to make it happen.

Yet, with all of my mother's passion for promoting people, she never believed in giving a false compliment. When we were together and she heard me compliment someone's dinner, she would later ask me, "Did you really like it?" I would say, "Well, not really, yet she tried so hard to make dinner, I wanted to make her feel good."

My mother would say, "I did not say anything about the food, because I don't believe in giving a false compliment." She clearly heard people, sized them up, yet would only acknowledge what was true.

"Cap daya fa hasdaya."
(Russian quote from her father)
Translation: "Respect him but be suspicious."

Mom loved people. But she was very careful about what she shared about herself. Perhaps it was due to small-town dynamics, where gossip energized the daily routine, or perhaps it was due to her focus on projecting the positive. Whatever it was, Mom would rarely, if at all, tell any person outside the family anything negative, sad, or worrisome in her life.

She had had CLL for ten years before she told anyone outside of the family about it. "If you have a problem," she would say to me, "only discuss it with family!"

"Not everything that shines is gold."

She was following her own advice. She chose very carefully what she told people about herself, stressing only the upbeat, ensuring her story was told by her own words and actions.

Indeed, her two sisters did the same. This practice came from their father, a man who worked so hard as an immigrant to build his life and take care of his family, and who was determined to be in charge of his own narrative. It was a lesson that Mom embraced.

4. Be your best at all times— and don't be a perfectionist

Mom's advice about doing your best:

- Pay attention to your appearance.

- Be organized.

- Use your time constructively.

- Don't be hard on yourself.

- Enjoy the feeling of doing your best.

"Look your best. Who said love is blind?"

For my mother, one of the ways to inspire her to "be your best" was to "look your best."

I cannot remember a time when my mother left home without making sure she looked "put together," no matter where she was going. Even if it was just a quick drive to the supermarket for a missing ingredient halfway through baking a cake, Mom would pause it all, with batter up to her elbows and egg whites in the mixer, to wash up, change her clothes, put on lipstick, and style her hair all for an extra bit of baking powder.

When I was a child, I was perplexed by that behavior. It felt oddly formal to me. Why couldn't she just run a quick brush through her hair, run out of the house, and just be herself? Even though I was proud of my mother's good looks, I could not understand why she was not more casual about what she looked like and why she took such time on her face, hair, and clothes. Looking back on my mother's considered attention to her considerable appearance, it is clearer to me. Her disciplined attention to looking her best was driven by her desire to do her best. It was inherent in my mother's makeup, inside and out. Mom understood the value of the "public face," carefully honed and consistently shaped.

She knew her appearance would have an impact on the way people perceived her—and how people perceived her did reinforce her ability to get things done. The way she appeared on the outside reflected the resolve and competency on the inside. Being seen as put together

conveyed the message that she had her life together—
even at the end.

My mother died in Florida. On the last Monday of her
life, she urged my father to deal with skin surgery he
had put off for months. He reluctantly agreed to a day-
long procedure, and unfortunately the appointment
took place on a day that my mother's condition was to
severely weaken. I called my cousin Ron in Florida and
asked him to check up on my mother. Ron lived a block
away and, like so many others, he had a special, close
relationship to my mother. They talked every day. She
respected Ron's work ethic and was proud of his success.
They shared a similar approach to life—to avoid complaining and just take action.

As Ron tells the story, he walked in the condo that day
and saw my mother lying on a chaise in the corner of
her shaded veranda, overlooking the water. It was her
favorite place to sit and watch the clouds as the sun rose
over the water. Ron saw my mother's condition: she was
failing. He knew he had to get her to an emergency room
immediately. She was extremely resistant, but at his quiet
insistence, she finally agreed. She was having problems
breathing, it was difficult to walk, and as she got up

slowly to leave for the hospital, she turned to my cousin and said, "Let me first put on my makeup." Two days later she died.

Even at the end, my mother understood the power of a public persona. I have worked in the PR business for decades studying ways to shape and sharpen images and now realize how my mother's "look" created her "brand." Not unlike "Intel inside," it was the "Pauly outside" that stood for something special. Her carefully crafted appearance communicated that she was a woman of presence not easily ignored.

This presence belied her size. Mom was a small 5'2", thin, and pretty in both a dramatic and cute kind of way. She had a signature hairstyle, bright blond hair that was cut very short, with a wedge in the back and a big swooping wave in front. She cut her hair into this style—after emerging from the '60s flip—sometime during the late 1970s and never changed her hairstyle again. The sweeping wave over her forehead suited her so well. It highlighted her bright blue eyes, framed her large smile, and made her look approachable and formidable at the same time. She got her hair done twice a week, so it always looked perfectly well shaped, with no hair out of place.

Suits were her other trademark. They were an essential element of the Pauly look. When she would visit me when I lived in New Rochelle, New York, she would always plan to go to Reiman's, a store that sold designer suits at discount.

I think Mom's motivation to visit New Rochelle was influenced as much by Reiman's as by wanting to see my children and me. It actually took me a year or two to realize that. It was sometime in the late 1980s. My mother and I would be sitting in the family room, talking and playing with my children, completely engaged in the moment—and she would say casually, almost as a second thought, "Why don't we go to Reiman's now?"

We would then leave the kids with a babysitter and make the expedition. She bought many beautifully designed suits that she would wear at her board meetings, ensuring that she would stand out for her appearance as well as her ideas. Her suits made a statement about her confidence and projected her ability to get things done. She chose bright colors—strong purple, deep green, burgundy red—with matching, intricately patterned, striking silk blouses. She would line up her suits in her closet, ordered by color, as if they were briefs in a file, waiting to be used to make her point.

After Reiman's closed, she discovered St. John suits, and later in her sixties and seventies those suits defined her style. She accumulated many suits during the years, with matching skirts, pants, and jackets in bright powder blues, sunny yellows, and mint greens that exuded a powerful joy. She was a woman to be noticed.

With her signature blond hair style and distinctive suits, she presented herself as a woman who gave her best effort to get things done. Perception was truth. She expressed that truth to us many times.

"Give your best effort in all you do."

It seemed a simple piece of advice—do your best—but Mom made it something more. It became not just about what was accomplished but also the attitude to getting there. Mom repeatedly advised my brother, my children, and me that whatever we did, we must be one hundred percent devoted to the task. It was the amount of concentrated effort that was important to her, more than the result. She had little tolerance for doing things halfway.

The energy invested in doing your best strengthened the bond with my father. My father loved his work. This work ethic, striving for achievement, doing your best was a core of the respect that knit them together, and it became the fabric of our family.

> *"If you are going to do something,*
> *then do it right—or don't do it at all."*

Mom had a special appreciation for anyone who took a job seriously. It was less about the job they did than how they did the job. It taught me to respect people's work regardless of whether it was attached to a college degree. She respected others when they respected themselves and took pride in what they did.

She taught us that lesson at a young age. When my brother and I were young, living in the house in West Pittston, we were expected to do chores around the house, particularly on the weekends. As she gave us our tasks, Mom would ensure we would not do things halfway. I can still hear my mother saying, "Don't just move that dust cloth around—really clean it. If you are going to do a job, then do it well. Give it everything you have." The committed action in and of itself would give the task a meaning, no matter what we were doing.

"Order enables a life. Get organized."

There was a disciplined approach to doing your best and a process to getting there. My mother knew how to use order to enhance her ability to do her best in whatever she was doing.

Just two summers ago, when I was leaving home to attend a wedding, I grabbed an elegant black bag from the shelf. It had been my mother's. When I opened the bag to put in my lipstick, I found her presence. In the bag were several neatly placed items: her hanky, her antiseptic hand cleaner, her small comb, and some mints. I was struck by the fact that the hand cleaner was just the right size, perfect for the small purse. I imagined that she had once set out to the store to find that very cleaner, in the perfect size, and made sure all her purses had them, ready to go for any special occasion.

Her sense of order carried through all aspects of her life. Her drawers were arranged with containers and organizers. No pen or pencil was alone, but in packs in containers. In her closet, the purses were lined up, and her sweaters all faced the same way and all hung on same-colored hangers.

Likewise, all her important papers were in her safe or filed in the folders she kept in a Lucite file rack by the desk in her bedroom. That way, each of the many non-profit organizations she chaired had its own folder, containing plans, committees, programs, and lists. She kept a trail of correspondence and notes that shaped her task plan, with dates for follow-up and action.

Mom kept her phone numbers, calendar, and to-do list updated and organized daily. She had organized her frequently called numbers in books alphabetically and included everyone from the favorite restaurants to her hairdresser, each written with clear, strong handwriting. This order empowered her.

Mom bought calendars with months that had large spaces for each day so she could write and plan on her calendar all the events and appointments in her life. Whenever I came home to visit—whether from college, from graduate school, as a young married woman, or later as a single mom—it did not matter how old or busy

I was; I always loved to lie on her bed, next to her, hold her hand, and read the calendar. Her life seemed so full. Every day in her book was full, with dates for parties, dinners with friends, board meetings for her organizations, bridge, golf, and tennis. Each day, like each of her efforts, seemed filled to the fullest. It represented an order to me that somehow guarded against the randomness of life.

One of my favorite ways that my mother kept the order of her life was in her scrapbooks. She must have had at least six of them, each containing the many news clippings in which she appeared. The clippings tracked her career as a volunteer in the community, from her first work for Heart Association and Pittston Hospital to her leadership restructuring visiting nurses associations into home health services, and her many awards in the community that recognized her contributions as a volunteer. Since my mother often did the volunteer PR for these organizations, she understood the value of a photograph as a way to energize and commit people to do a volunteer job. So there were literally hundreds of pictures of Mom with her friends through the years, at hundreds of her committee meetings documented in the local papers. She cut and pasted these articles in the scrapbooks, shaping a record of her life, claiming it through her order and creation.

This order provided a framework that shaped the way my mother approached time. She believed that time is not just passing through us or around us; it has to be used. We learned that lesson very early. When we were growing up, Mom would not let my brother and me sleep past 7:30 on the weekends, ever. Despite our protests, groaning that we were tired, particularly in our teens, it never mattered. We were woken up early, with a loud good morning, followed quickly by, "It's time to be constructive."

As a child, I was not sure what that meant, outside of doing the chores Mom had in mind for that day, but as I grew older and watched my mother live her life, with her volunteering, child rearing, and friendships, the lesson seems to have now been deeply embedded in my brother and me. Rarely do days go by for the both of us, now, in our late fifties, when we spend them without a project, a focus, a goal to accomplish. It's as if my mother's urging us through our childhoods to be constructive, take on a task, and do something fully was a gift she gave us to realize ourselves.

However, I do admit to taking my mother's advice to the extreme. As a student and an adult, I not only worked hard to give the best effort; I expected total perfectionism. It was as if I had taken my mother's advice to the exponential, scrutinizing results, questioning the levels of perfection in everything I did. My own doubting betrayed the fear that my best was never good enough.

Not so with Mom. This questioning appeared not to have afflicted her. She had no conflicted feelings about value of the result. She just gave herself to the task. The effort was the meaning, freeing her to do her best.

5. Be proud of your religion— and respect all religions

Mom's advice on religion

- Take part.

- Shape actions based on its values.

- Enjoy the holidays and the food.

- Be interested in other religions and promote understanding of new religions.

- Leave room in your life for the spiritual.

> *"There is depth to our existence.*
> *God is within us."*

When I was a young girl and asked Mom if she believed in God, she would answer my question by describing the story of her boyfriend Butch, whom she met at Penn State a year before she met my father. She would describe Butch as the intellectual, the poet, the daring dreamer who rode a motorcycle. Although she would never make the comparison, I would visualize him in stark contrast to my father, the pragmatist and businessman.

After she would mention Butch, I would look for him among her Penn State college pictures that she had pasted on every page in a brown album whose bindings were then frayed and crumbling. As my mother would point him out, I was surprised that I could never quite see his face. The one small picture of Butch, standing by his motorcycle, looked faded and gray, opposite the large photo of my father, lying on his side in a park at Penn State, in a suit, open collar, pipe in his hand, handsome, looking up at my mother, broadly smiling.

Mom told me that she and Butch, after much questioning about the existence of God, decided to visit all the different churches in the community—Catholic, Methodist, Episcopalian, Baptist. . . whatever large or small church they could find—and they would attend services there, listen to the ministers, and read their prayer books. After what may have been a three-month spiritual search, she told me that she and Butch decided to become deists, which meant they believed in God but were not sure about the value of any religion.

According to my mother, this deist period lasted about another month. When her parents learned she was visiting churches with Butch, they sent her sister Marcella to college to check up on her. Although Mom did not provide the details, I gather that soon after that visit and some serious talks with Marcella, both the deist and Butch period ended quite quickly and without much remorse.

Still, I believe that her spiritual search never ended. In fact, the search underpinned the quality of her life. It would reach the surface in her wide embrace of people, in her full awareness of the moments in a day, and in her ability to find the joy in the routine of living.

"How we find the presence of God is how we approach our behavior and actions."

Despite her early deist beliefs, and although not particularly religious, my mother raised my brother and me to know the importance of being Jewish and to live its values. She talked about how Jewish belief was centered on action.

Deeds lived on, and what linked them together was the

chain of connections. My mother taught us in ways large and small how our participation in our religion keeps us connected to our family, our larger community, and ourselves.

For my mother, Judaism was about connections. When she and my father married and settled in West Pittston in the early 1950s, she had little choice but to be connected to the one small synagogue, known as Adith Achim, located on the other side of the Susquehanna River in Pittston.

The synagogue needed members. Not many Jews were settling in the coal-mining town in northeastern Pennsylvania then. Indeed, there were only fifty Jewish families when my parents moved to town. My parents' claim to fame was that they were the youngest Jewish couple to move to West Pittston, and in the next sixty years, they never lost that title.

Since the Jewish community was so small, all the denominations of Judaism—Orthodox, Conservative, and Reform—were found in the one small synagogue wedged narrowly between two apartment buildings on a hill. It was barely visible from the street, but it was the center of Jewish life in the small town. Mom felt a responsibility to get involved. I doubt she had a choice.

She used her acting and theater skills to produce original musicals for the sisterhood; I remember going to rehearsals in the synagogue basement rec room, where she would be directing her friends Gladys, Beverly, Lois, and Rita, housewives in West Pittston dressed up liked Annie Oakley for their new singing roles.

She signed us up for Hebrew school two days a week and on Sunday. There was no negotiation about going. Since we were small in number in the classes, four to five Jewish children in our age group, there also was no hiding. We all had to participate. Our sense of identity emerged from those early years. Mom would emphasize to my brother and me that we had a responsibility to be Jewish.

The small synagogue was a rotating platform for rabbis who were looking for an undemanding first pulpit experience. They would stay a few years and move on. The synagogue closed when I was fourteen, but as far as I remembered, there were a least a half a dozen odd rabbis coming and going—the comedian Jackie Mason's brother, a rabbi who could not speak, another rabbi who did not know how to stop speaking, a rabbi from Israel who did not want to be a rabbi but did not know what else to do.

Our rabbis were fleeting but the fifty families were consistent. Each family would have its own pew, and for each of the Jewish holidays, the pews would fill up with the family members, each in their own rows that would never change. My mother and father would sit with my father's parents, and we next to them in the fifth-row pew, year in and year out. The pew arrangement provided a sense of continuity that, even now after all these years, I feel a comfort in that is hard to describe. The only reason people left the synagogue was their death. In fact, now when I go to the small Jewish cemetery on the outskirts of West Pittston, wedged near old mounds of coal to visit my mother's grave, I see the names of the members of the synagogue, etched in the tombstones, near her. They are lined up still, in their never changing rows.

For the Jewish New Year that we celebrated at the Pittston synagogue, my brother, mother, and I would walk to my grandmother's house, a few blocks away from ours on the shore of the Susquehanna River. Then we would walk together over the bridge from West Pittston to Pittston and up the hill to the synagogue. Although we were not Orthodox Jews, we would always walk on the holidays. My mother would ensure that my brother and I had new clothes for the New Year, which we would first put on that day. The walk would be slow, because of the new shoes that would inevitably pinch. We would walk along the riverbank on Susquehanna Avenue, where the leaves on the cherry trees were turning yellow. As we walked, Rob, Mom, and I would pick up chestnuts still in their green prickly shells, and then we would open up the shells to discover the shiny brown chestnut, new like our shoes and clothes. The three of us would keep them in our pockets for the service, passing them to each other as everyone prayed.

"God is in us as we do good for others."

The small town connected us to Judaism, but it was food and family that forged the strongest connection. It was at home, at the dinner table, where my mother gave Judaism a deeper meaning in our lives.

Up to two months before the high holy days of Rosh Hashonah and Yom Kippur, and for Passover, Mom would begin talking about the menu, the guests, and the details of the day. She would go through the menu with me and plan the dinner in intricate detail, and on the day itself, the table would be beautifully set with flowers, her crystal, and china. The menu was the same every year, so it was always amusing to go through the same menu in great detail every year. Still it was part of the ritual to talk about the menu—so we did.

We talked and she would cook it all: gefilte fish, chicken soup with her matzo balls, brisket, chicken, stuffed cabbage, stewed fruit, Jell-O mold—all at one dinner. Her food was like the ancient temple offerings, given with her full-hearted effort and love and devotion to her family.

In addition to the food, Mom made sure to think about the special message for the holidays that she would impart each year before we fell into a daze after eating all her food. This past year when I opened the Passover Haggadah for the Seder, I found one of those messages she had written folded on a piece of paper inside.

"The Passover holiday perhaps best symbolizes what all Jewish festivals are about—home and children, family and friends—traditions and food, song and laughter, values and teachings. It's a time when Jews remind

themselves that whenever anyone is enslaved anywhere in the world, no one is really free and that each of us has a responsibility to work for the freedom of every human being."

At the holidays, she would gather us in her home in West Pittston and later in Kingston, along with her parents, Dad's parents, her sisters, their husbands, their children, my cousins. There were often eighteen to twenty people at the house. Generations of the family sat around our table, the food and ritual binding us to each other.

Mom would put her mark on the traditions as well. My father's family had a ritual for Passover that my mother adapted one year. Each year after the Seder readings concluded and right before the start of dinner, we would enthusiastically engage in my father's family tradition: the egg fight. We would hold unblemished, uncracked hard boiled eggs and each of us would try to crack each other's egg, using our egg as a weapon.

I don't know how the tradition got started or why my father's great grandfather on his mother's side decided to engage in egg cracking. But it became a highly competitive way perhaps to reinforce that we were free. The person whose egg remained uncracked throughout the competition was declared a winner and everyone would then quickly eat the eggs, because we were very hungry after waiting an hour and a half throughout the service. It was a tough fight and my father typically won to much applause and envy. But one year the competition was different. Mom decided to put a raw egg into the mix. Uncle Bernie got the raw egg and none of us ever forgot it. Perhaps it was her way of saying that with freedom, you never know what to expect.

After her parents and my father's parents died, and her sisters no longer came to Seder, mom would mix up the group with her friends, people who were alone, and people who were Christian, ministers, nuns and priests whom she would meet at her board meetings and with whom she had become dear friends.

It was especially interesting that my mother was so open to learning about other religions because growing up in a small town and being a small community of Jews, we did not experience high levels of tolerance, especially when my brother and I were young.

I remember walking home from grade school with my

friends and the conversation turned to the fact that Jews did not believe in Jesus and that there was something hugely wrong with me for believing that. I remember running home, feeling both angry and frightened. When I told my mother, she responded simply and calmly, "Be proud of your history, heritage, and religion." It was her refrain.

She said, "People who took their religion seriously would respect that we also took our religion seriously."

Instead of turning the hurt of anti-Semitism into anger, my mother transformed it into an opportunity for outreach and learning. Her many friendships with nuns, priests, and ministers in the community were typical of her individualized, interfaith relations. She would find something familiar in their personality, character, work ethic, or sense of humor, and based on this commonality, they would become good friends. Mom would be impressed with a particular monsignor's intelligence and commitment to the community, and the next thing we knew he was at our Seder. Then the next thing we knew, Mom was joining a board in his parish or an advisory committee of Catholic colleges in the community.

Mom cut through the barriers of small-town intolerance and stereotypes through her sheer pleasure in people and her natural curiosity about their lives.

This was typical. Being my mother, she encountered the negative with the positive. Mon wanted us to strongly identify with Judaism, but she never did it by attacking anyone else's religion. On the contrary, she appreciated and thoroughly enjoyed the diversity.

"The issue to be faced is: how to combine loyalty to one's own tradition with reverence for different traditions."

My mother helped organize the interfaith committee of the Wilkes Barre community and served on its board for many years. The interfaith committee visited all the churches, mosques, and synagogues in the area. She loved the visits. Despite being a former deist, my mother would attend all the different tours and afterward would call me enthusiastically to let me know how much fun the Baptists were.

Her work with the Catholic community extended to helping launch the Ethics Institute of Northeast Pennsylvania with her close friend Sister Sienna, of the Sisters of Mercy. My mother met Sister Sienna when she chaired the art gallery at Miseracorida University, a Catholic university in the community. Sister Sienna was a professor there, and the two of them clicked. They could not have been more different. Sister Sienna had taken the vow of poverty as a nun when she was eighteen. My mother was a glamorous-looking blond who loved jewelry and clothes. They struck a bond of devotion and support, recognizing in each other the same spiritual face and proving the power of interfaith living by their very friendship.

Together they launched the Ethics Institute in an effort to initiate conversations about ethics in the community. Based at the Misericorida University and involving academic, business, and nonprofit leaders, it developed ways to bring the discussion of ethics into the issues impacting the community, such as employment, politics, or health care. Mom thought the question of ethics was a discussion for the family too. She cut out the following quote to generate conversation among us. During dinner, we had to discuss the answer to these questions. She sent them on to me and suggested that they be the subject of my dinner parties, and when I was dating after my divorce, she said to me, "Did you ask him the ethics questions?"

Ethics tries to resolve value conflicts: How do you determine your values? Ask yourself:

1. What do you do with your money?
2. What do you do with your free time?
3. What do you do with your friends?

Mom's interfaith and ethics work reflected what she first imparted to my brother and me about the values of religion. Deeds define character. That is what lives on after we are gone.

6. Be funny—and do not laugh at jokes that undermine you

ॐ

Mom's advice:

- Focus on what's funny.

- Don't take yourself seriously.

- But don't tolerate jokes that put you down.

Mom loved to laugh—big, uproarious, head thrown back, wide, huge laughter. She was funny and consistently saw the humor in life. It was reflected in how she was a center of energy in the family and among her friends, all of us seeking her good conversation, funny commentary, great stories, and, of course, laughter.

"Laughter is universal and we or at least most of us don't need lessons. We don't need experts to tell us that laughter reduces tension, clears the mind, and lifts the spirits. A good laugh is a kind of

77

workout. It's not exactly a calorie-burner—
you can laugh yourself silly, yet it does help move
nutrients and oxygen along to the bodies' tissues.
That might be one reason why a fit of mirth
makes people feel better. Just avoid the kind of
laughing that causes someone else pain."

Mom would always say that you have to laugh at yourself—and find what is funny in life. She was an advocate of not taking herself too seriously. Her point was that if you have a sense of humor about yourself, it will lift you up.

She took her own advice.

A year before she died, Mom got really sick. She was weak from the chemo, tired, and in pain. Her doctor hospitalized her in a deteriorating hospital on the south side of Wilkes Barre. The walls were a dismal gray color of fatigue and loss. It was December, and it was gray outside, too, reflecting Wilkes Barre in the winter. Mom talked about hospice. We were all very frightened to see Mom so weak and thin, but Mom was not frightened. Mom was Mom.

Knowing that she may be near the end, she called her sister Florence to say goodbye. Rob and I were in the room with her when she sat up slowly in the bed and dialed my aunt's number. My aunt was not home, so she left a message in a quiet, steady voice, saying, "Florence, this is your baby sister. I want you to know I love you very much and just wanted to say goodbye—and by the way, please don't call back."

She hung up the phone, and the absurdity of the message overwhelmed us. We all burst into laughter and suddenly in the laughter the fear was gone.

Over the next few days, my children and Rob's wife at the time, Allison, joined my brother, father, and me at the hospital. As we each spent time with her to say good-bye, my mother took this opportunity to do what she loved to do—give advice. As she spoke with each of us, she made it seem like it was going to be her final piece of wisdom. We listened closely. Rob and Allison came together, and Mom held both their hands. She told them to be good to each other.

She then met with my children and talked with them about each of their talents in a way that showed that she really knew their true nature. She reminded them to take care of each other. Then she turned to me and said, "And my final advice to you is, make sure you put all your left-over food in Tupperware containers; don't use glass bowls."

Mom's sense of the absurd kept us laughing. She went home a week later, recovered, and spent the winter in Florida.

Of course, April Fool's Day was one of her favorite holidays. She loved to tell April Fool's jokes to my brother and me when we were children, and she would keep it up long after we had moved out of the house and had children of our own. No matter what day of the week April Fool's Day fell on, at 6:30 in the morning, the phone would ring and there would be Mom saying, "The electricity is out and I cannot find your father," or "Surprise, we decided to visit you and are outside your front door," or "We have just won a prize and are going to Europe the next day." Whatever it was, since it was the first call of the morning, we would believe her and she would say, "April Fool's!" and burst out laughing. There was not one April Fool's Day that she missed. It gave her an excuse to wake us up with laughter.

But it was her famous lemon meringue pie that showed her love for the absurd. Mom would spend many hours making a lemon meringue pie and would do so only rarely, usually just for Thanksgiving. She would make the crust first, then the lemon filling, and then beat the egg whites and sugar into astoundingly beautiful white peaks that she would then toast to a mahogany brown. After our Thanksgiving meal, she would make a major entrance into the dining room, apron tied at her waist, holding the lemon meringue aloft to receive our "oohs" and "ahs" of gratitude and praise.

As part of the Thanksgiving tradition, my father would then take the pie in the palm of his hand and begin to swing it up and down, pretending that he was going to throw it in my brother's face. We would, all of us around the table—grandparents, aunts, uncles, and cousins— look in horror at my father's behavior, thinking how could he even pretend that there would be such a devastating end to such a beautiful dessert? Dad would then place the pie down, and Mom would proceed to cut us all pieces. This lemon meringue pie ritual went on for at least three years.

Then, one Thanksgiving, as Dad raised Mom's pie

and pretended to throw it into my brother's face, my mother quickly grabbed the pie from my father's hand, saying, "I am tired of this joke every year!" We never expected her next move when she shoved the pie into my brother's face. Everyone around the table burst into laughter after we recovered from the shock of the loss of that pie. Yet, to this day, I don't think my brother has recovered.

The times my mother would not laugh were at jokes that tore people down. My mother saw a clear difference between being self-deprecating and not taking yourself so seriously, and someone using the façade of humor to denigrate someone else.

She would recognize it around her and tell me, "I love to laugh, but I will never laugh at a joke that tears me down. That's not funny."

She used to frequently quote her close friend Albert, a physician who lived and practiced across the river in Pittston. He was at least fifteen years older than my mother, but they had a strong friendship. He was her mentor and stock market friend during her early married life. They would get on the phone in the morning and discuss different stock market trades they would make during the day. My mother trusted Albert's honest advice in stocks, and also in life.

She told me that once over dinner with my father, Albert and his wife, and some other friends, someone made a joke that was at the expense of my mother. "As I started to laugh," she said, "Albert grabbed my arm and said to me without any humor at all, 'Never laugh at a joke that aims to cut you down. These jokes are nothing to laugh at. Feel free to make fun of yourself, but don't tolerate the other kind.'" She told that story many times to me, emphasizing the use of humor to lift up not tear down.

7. Be connected to nature— and stay connected

క్రిల్

Mom's advice:

- Take the time to connect with nature.

- Do that repeatedly.

> *"Perhaps the truth depends upon*
> *a walk around the lake."*

My mother taught me to be in touch with nature, just as her father had taught her.

As a girl, Mom spent summers at my grandfather's cottage on Chapman Lake, a small lake near the northern outskirts of Scranton, Pennsylvania. Every summer my grandparents would move up there, and through childhood and their teen years, my mother and her sisters would spend days with their friends, sitting on the docks that jutted out into the lake. I would romanticize her stories as portraits of perfect summer days.

As Mom told me the stories, she would bring out her photo album from high school, which was full of carefully pasted pictures of her friends. She would run through the pictures as she told me about lying on the docks, meeting boys, swimming in the cold lake, and laughing her with sisters. As a young girl, I would inhale these pictures, examining closely the faces of Mom and her friends, all of whom conveyed a sunny radiance of expectation. Those summers showed Mom looking feisty and funny, mugging for the camera in her 1940s bathing suits with her friends Shirley, Sarita, and Marilyn.

Her stories became imprinted on me. Chapman Lake became a part of our family's collective memory, because it began our love affair with nature.

"Look deep into nature, and then you will understand everything better."

Every summer, up until high school, my brother and I and our four cousins would visit our grandparents at Chapman Lake during the weekends. My grandfather owned a cottage that was built for two families, with one small home on each side of the cottage. On my grandparents' side were two bedrooms just large enough to fit a double bed in each, a small living room with one worn couch and two chairs, and a basic practical kitchen where my brother and I would watch my grandmother prepare dinner at her red and chrome kitchen table.

In front of the cottage was a wide, screened-in porch that spanned its length. There, on a wicker table, my grandmother would serve her special lunches of blintzes. The front porch was framed by two magnificent hydrangea bushes that reached nearly the roof of the cottage and where there are many pictures of my brother and me dressed in twin outfits in the late 1950s.

One side of my grandfather's front yard was rimmed with layers of vines of raspberry and blackberries that we would run to pick as soon as my mother's car reached the front lawn of the cottage. In the backyard was a large garden, with five distinct cultivated areas of vegetables, herbs, and fruit that my grandfather had lovingly planted, nurtured, and pruned. Around the garden, he had planted several fruit trees that circled twelve tall poplar and white birch trees that he described not as trees, but as the twelve tribes of Israel.

He never called his garden a garden either. It was his "farm." There were many rituals associated with the "farm." As soon as my mother, brother, and I would arrive on a Sunday (my father would arrive later because he spent most of Sunday working at the store), my grandfather would greet us, and before we had time to eat the raspberries from the bushes, he would pull us to him and say, "Come, see the farm."

Bobby would take my mother's arm, and my brother and I would follow. It was a slow, deliberate walk. My grandfather would talk to my mother about the progress of every seed he had planted, pointing out the details of its growth. My brother and I could not stray away to grab extra raspberries and blackberries; we had to stay on the walk and listen.

Bobby would show us the gooseberry and current bushes and make us touch the gooseberry branches to see the sharp, long prickers near the fruit, and then he would pluck two large, light pink gooseberries for my brother and me to taste. My mother would walk with him, holding hands and praising every detail of the property. "Look how large the tomatoes are," she would say. "Look at how perfect the edges of the garden are trimmed!" "Smell how good it all smells!" And we would smell the sweet fragrance of the moment connecting us.

Side by side with Bobby, we would walk through the garden and consider every vegetable. Bobby would stop at an area filled with straggly, large, slowly browning green leaves. He would say, "Look . . . isn't it magnificent?" He would tell us to bend down and slowly pull the leaves. As we did, a bouquet of small brown potatoes would emerge. He told us to run to the kitchen in the cottage and give them to our grandmother so she could boil them quickly with the skins on. "How can we possibly eat the skins?" I asked in my concerned, ten-year-old voice. He said, "It's totally fresh and natural and full of what is precious in the earth."

As my grandmother cooked the new potatoes (to be eaten with a bit of butter ten minutes later), he would continue the examination—as if we never saw his garden the previous week before. We would stop to admire the cucumbers, and he would show us how to find small ones under the yellow flowers. He would pick it, wipe away the dirt, pull out a saltshaker from his pocket, and salt the cucumber quickly—"not too much; salt is poison"— then he would tell us to eat it on the spot.

Mom would then tell us that Bobby was a source of wisdom—way ahead of his time—for what was fresh, natural, and good for us. Bobby would then lead us to his peach and plum trees behind the vegetable plots, explaining in great detail that they were very difficult to grow, that it took time for the trees to bear fruit, and that nature had a way of teaching us patience.

My grandfather transplanted some bushes and trees from his "farm" into my mother's yard when we lived in West Pittston, and she continued in his tradition of not just looking at a tree but praising it. One of my mother's favorites was the magnolia tree that grew rapidly and profusely with hundreds of magnolia flowers every spring. Every day in May, Mom would have my brother and me examine the tree just when the buds were beginning to form until the tree bloomed its glorious pink flowers. Every spring Mom would take pictures of us, mapping our lives through its seasons. To this day, I can still see those big buds folded onto themselves and then remember as they slowly opened to show the pink edging on the tips of each fold.

Even as an adult, each time I would visit her home, we would have to walk around the yard where she examined each bush, the unusual tree, and the birds that would visit in her birdbath. She loved the weeping cherry tree by her bedroom window, and when it bloomed, she would call me on the phone to give me the news.

What Bobby taught my mother, she taught us. She taught us to slow down, to smell, taste, and appreciate the beauty around us. She wanted to teach us what gave her such an unmovable core of happiness.

She taught us as well to respect people who planted and worked the soil—and to be sensitive to what was fresh and reflected the season. She made us notice. Before farmer's markets were so popular, my mother discovered farm stands and knew all the local farmers. Going to the farm stand with her was always a journey to bounty. She would find small, hidden stands close to the shores of the Susquehanna River where crops grew. As she approached the stand, the owner would look carefully at the crops and pick out what was the best, the sweetest, the freshest for her. Mom would have a conversation with everyone about when the corn was picked or how the tomatoes were doing this year. She conveyed to us that these conversations were a priority. We had to stop and fully appreciate it all.

"Let nature be your teacher."

Mom's connection to nature came from her connection to her father. These connections bind my brother and me still. Looking back at that small cottage at Chapman Lake, I see how little and bare that cottage really was. But of course no matter what the size of the cottage, it was tiny compared to the expanse and intricate wonder outside its doors.

What I now remember most is the beauty of my grandfather's large ripe tomatoes, the rustling of the leaves in the warm wind of a Sunday afternoon, sitting with my grandfather and mother on chaise lounges at his "farm," and leaning against my mother to tip back my head and watch the clouds drift in the sky.

Now, both my brother and I have found houses situated in the country. I think of how my grandfather would have viewed these homes as incidental to what is around them. And I see it too. It is not the homes we are after but the feeling you get from the shape of the sweeping weeping willow tree.

Nature is more than memory. In teaching me to really look at natural beauty, my mother helped me to connect to the knowledge that life exceeds our knowing.

My mother kept many plants in her house and had a knack for growing African violets and interesting flowering cactus plants, all of which she would keep in the trestle at the landing of the stairs that led to the basement. Many times she would have more than a dozen African violets of all colors in bloom, a mosaic of accomplishment.

Like the plants in her yard, they were always worthy of praise. When we visited her, she would take us to the landing of the stairs and review in detail the status of different African violet varieties, noticing which budded easily, which bloom had surprised her with its hardiness, and which had an unusual color.

She kept various African violets in bloom for at least ten years. When she left for Florida as she did every winter, she typically cleared out most of the plants to begin the process of nurturing the African violets when she returned. The last time she left for Florida, right before her death, she left one plant. We saw it when we returned from Florida for my mother's funeral. The plant sitting alone on the trellis was flowerless and drooping. I am sure my mother simply forgot to throw it out. Yet, one week later, somehow reassuringly, the plant bloomed.

8. Be a giver—and set limits

ॐ

Mom's advice on giving:

- Concentrate on love.

- Make giving a priority.

- Do not use giving to escape from yourself.

"To love and be loved is everything."

My mother had many ways to sustain a happy, upbeat attitude, but what kept her positive life together was her deep capacity to love. Giving was love in action. For my mother, to give was to live and to live was to give.

"Love is giving, not taking. It wants the best for the one you love. Love makes you want to charge out into the world and DO, as well as THINK, big."

My father, brother, and I were the lucky recipients of her

giving, but she also taught us that giving should enhance a life, not overwhelm it. Giving was not an escape from facing yourself; it was a way to realize yourself.

Family is first.

My brother would often say to me, "Mom could have done anything—run a large company, be an executive at a nonprofit agency. She could have had any career, but what she wanted to do more than anything was give to her family."

That was true. Dad was her center, and we knew it. Their relationship was one of love and respect, caring and laughter, chemistry and appreciation, right until the last day of my mother's life when my father could not leave her side. Mom gave to my father, by thinking of his needs and meeting them. He was her priority, and she paid attention to the details of caring for him. When my father decided he wanted to learn to play tennis, so did my mother. When he decided next to try golf, so did my mother. When my father had a heart attack and had to change his diet to focus on low fat and no red meats, my mother made it her mission to change how she cooked. She watched out for his health, his diet, his happiness.

She catered to my father's needs, but throughout, she always had a strong sense of herself and her limits.

My parents also gave each other a lot of room to live on their own. Dad's occupation was his preoccupation. He gave his business most of his attention, while my mother carved out her own life in her organizations and volunteering. They enabled each other to grow and evolve by not being each other's sole focus and not demanding it.

After my father, my mother devoted her time to my brother and me in a way that made each of us feel understood. My mother never hesitated to tell us that she was proud of us, from when we were children in our individual accomplishments and later throughout our adult lives. My brother and I always had the sense that when my mother woke up and started her day, we were her focus, her preoccupation. My mother always told me, "I love being a mother." Her parenting never felt too anxious or nervous; in fact, she had a way to minimize life's stress and solve problems in a smart and calm way. No matter what I was going through in my life, I never felt my mother incessantly worried. Rather, she conveyed a calm assurance that life would work out and we had the capabilities to make it so.

Yet, she was still involved in the many details of our lives. When we were children, she wanted to know our friends, get involved in our activities, know the things that were bothering us, and make sure she was involved somehow. She often said she got her best ideas in the middle of the night, thinking of ways to make things easier, stronger for us all. I would call her about a problem, and she would never hesitate to give me her advice and ideas for solutions. She was my strongest supporter and guide.

My brother felt the same way. When my brother, who was always in the family business, decided that he also wanted to open a jazz and blues club in the area, the family was not particularly supportive. My parents thought it would take time away from his main occupation, but when my brother decided to move forward with it, my mother was right in the middle of it, helping him decorate, buying paintings she saw of jazz singers, giving advice on menus, guiding the chefs at the club, and promoting the club to all her friends, ensuring she could get a crowd for all the big concerts. She offered the jazz club as a venue for fundraisers for her nonprofit organizations and became one its stalwart fans. If it was important to my brother, it became important to my mother.

Mom concentrated on us, thought a lot about our lives, and gave us a lot of advice, whether we were willing to hear it or not. I can still hear her saying, "I am giving you my opinion—and of course I have your best interests at heart—so even if it's not what you want to hear, I am going to tell you anyway."

My mother never held back her opinions. She would frequently say, "You want me to tell you what I really think, right?" And before I could answer, she did.

She would often say to me, "I am so surprised that my friends don't readily give their honest opinions to their children." That would make me laugh, because Mom, of course, would never suspect that somehow we would not want her opinion. But I guess Mom at times would try to impose some restraint, because among her clips I found,

> *"Release me from trying to straighten out everyone's affairs!"*

Now reading it, I think "everyone" did not include her immediate family. Family affairs were central to her mission. She focused on her grandchildren with the same level of detail she had shown to her children. She was an influence on my daughter Lili, teaching her early on the value of giving and getting involved in the world around you. Once, when Mom was to receive a community award for her volunteer effort, I brought Lili, who was seven, to the award ceremony. My mother called up Lili to the podium and spoke to her in front of the entire gathered crowd about the value of giving to others. Lili stood by while she talked to the audience about Lili's own effort to gather clothes in her little red wagon for the victims of a hurricane in Jamaica. She was proud about what Lili had done.

She also held her accountable, even at seven, asking her to follow up to see what happened with the clothes she gathered and to find out what else she could do to help. She imparted both a love of giving and a responsibility to do it well.

In addition to her ideas, her opinions about giving, and her solutions to life's problems, Mom gave us her food.

Lots of it. Mom's food tasted like love. Garlic chicken, chicken strips, salad with garlic dressing, spaghetti and meatballs, veal Francaise, herb bread, brisket, stuffed cabbage, blueberry cobbler—these were her specialties.

And during my mother's last year of life, when she became increasingly weak and fatigued, staying at home for most of the day, she would center the day on the cooking so she could provide a dinner for my father. It was her way, I think, to not only do something creative that had a tangible result, but a way to keep on giving.

Outside our immediate family, Mom gave in ways where everyone also assumed they were the most special to her.

"Eleanor (Roosevelt) believed that happiness was not a goal but a byproduct of a life well lived. It comes from striving to help others find their happiness."

Five of my cousins, Deborah, Alice, Nancey, Ron, and Ron's wife Gail, each had a special relationship with my mother. She would go out of her way to regularly do something for each of them, taking the time to call them, send them gifts, and take an interest in their lives.

What is interesting to me is that each of my cousins was convinced that she or he had a special relationship with my mother that no one else could possibly have. She thought about them, cared about them, advocated for them in ways that took her beyond her day-to-day concerns. They felt the gift that Mom gave of making you feel that you were a special person in her life.

Strengthening the family and giving to the family, her sisters and brother-in-law and sister-in-law, Phil and Shiela, were central themes to her happiness. She also knew how to give to her friends in ways that cemented friendships. She listened, gave what people needed to receive, and made them feel special at the same time.

Giving in Friendships

"The sage does not accumulate for himself.
The more he uses for others, the more he has
for himself. The more he gives to others,
the more he possesses of his self."

Mom had many friends. When she started to spend several months in Florida in her late sixties, I was amazed at the wideness of the circle, the number of people who would call her in one day, how popular she was.

When she made plans to go out to dinner, every one of

her friends wanted to join. Often there would be eight to twelve people around the table, and Mom would have to demand, "One conversation, please." People wanted to be with her.

*"It's not possible in life
to make a selfish person happy."*

I can see all my mother's friends in my mind's eye—and how they changed over time, from her friends in her West Pittston days, to the Kingston friends, Florida friends, the golfing friends, the bridge friends, her volunteer friends, the board friends. There was no special type. Mom's innate interest in people went beyond friends who shared every interest with her. She appreciated the diversity of people from different religions, different parts of the country, different economic statuses. There seemed to be no barrier to her friendships. But I don't think I understood how much Mom gave to her friends until after she died.

She had a friend in the community, someone she knew from her volunteer life. I did not know her well at all, but when Mom was sick, Mom asked me to give a piece of jewelry to her friend Elly. I asked, "Why?" "She is a special person and a special person to me," she replied. So, after my mother died, I went to Elly's house for the first time, to give her the piece of jewelry Mom wanted her to have.

When I arrived at her home, I begin to realize the extent of their friendship. Elly brought me into the hall, and there hanging on the wall was a beautiful delicate lace handkerchief simply framed and displayed with prominence. She turned the frame over to show me a note attached:

> *"Dear Elly, I saw this beautiful handkerchief and it reminded me of the beauty of you."* —PAULY

Then Elly brought me into their dining room and showed me crystal Lennox candlesticks. "Your mother bought them for me when she asked me to introduce her at the Boy Scouts annual dinner, when she received their community leader award," Elly said. "I introduced many people at award ceremonies, but no one thought to buy me a gift except your mother." Elly then said to me, "I want to pass on the candles to you. Please save them and give them to Lili, your daughter, who has the same spirit of giving as your mother."

I thought of the way that my mother gave to Elly, someone with whom she had much respect and admiration, but someone who I did not even know was in her life. It was not the gifts my mother gave Elly that impacted me. It was something else, that almost indescribable quality of what my mother gave the best: recognition of who someone really was. That kind of understanding was a rare and elusive gift.

My mother was a giver, but she had her limits. If she felt someone was asking too much of her she would say no. I never saw her put herself in a position where the giving erased herself.

> "We need a brave examination of the codes of behavior that teach constant service, self-sacrifice, even effacement as the only acceptable models of behavior for women. We need to teach women to say, no. We need to help valiant women to know that they must be responsible and caring of themselves. Dr. Regina Kelly told the audience she was glad, 'I'm not as nice as I was in 1965.' I am glad, too—for myself."

I think Mom learned to set limits from her own mother, Lillian, who was the ultimate giver. My grandmother provided a home for her three daughters, Florence, Marcella, and Pauline, in a way where she always came last. Her husband made all the decisions—including what to make for dinner—giving her very little voice or any autonomy.

Mom was proud of her mother's giving, but angry and visibly annoyed by the self-sacrifice. She would mention how much her mother's overwhelming giving bothered her, and she was determined to stand up for herself and not assume the role of the invisible giver.

If she gave to family, friends, or relatives and her giving was not appreciated, she would stop. She was a firm believer that giving was not a one-way path. If she felt she was taken for granted in our nuclear family for whatever the reason—cooking, helping to solve a problem, going out of her way for errands—she would tell us so. My mother never used the face of self-sacrifice as a form of giving. Like so much else in her life, giving was entwined with the value of self-respect.

My mother loved people, emphasized to us the importance of giving of yourself to others, but she never allowed her giving to others to submerge herself.

9. Be involved in something larger than yourself—and stay involved

ॐ

Mom's advice on being involved:

- Find a way to volunteer.

- Whatever you give, you get ten-fold.

> *"If I am not for myself who will be. If I am only for myself, what am I and if not now when?"*

For my mother, being involved, forging connections, and taking action were like taking a daily breath. After wife and mother, volunteering was her particular and lasting identity. In fact, there are more quotes about volunteering and "giving back" in my mother's desk drawer than for any other subject.

She not only lived as a volunteer, she ensured that my brother and I understood its value. She spoke to us continually, especially when she was chairing different

nonprofit boards, that contributing your ideas and time
are what strengthens communities and ourselves. Being
only for yourself was an anathema for my mother. She
was not judgmental of people who did not get involved—
not usually, that is—but she made it clear to my brother,
her grandchildren, and me that if you were only for yourself, who really would you be? It was a message we could
not help but take seriously.

> *"The value of involvement—of volunteering—*
> *is a gift to your community, to your family*
> *and to yourself."*

Even now, despite a busy professional life, my mother's
words of get involved and make a difference are a steady
beat in my life. Often it has become a way to find my way.
When I feel a sense of loss or despair come upon me, I
tend, after years of training, not to go shopping but to
get involved , in something, in anything.

I remember so vividly the first Thanksgiving after my
divorce, when my children went with their father to the
meal. The sadness was tough to digest that day. I had an
invitation to a friend's house and went there so as not to
be alone. But before I went to her home, I knew I needed

to do something to lift the self pity out of range for a few hours. I went to the local hospital and volunteered to bring meals to patients.

That year, a hospital in New Rochelle, New York, happened to be a PR client. I knew the development director, so I called him. "Can you get me some time there?" I asked.

He made some calls, and for three hours, I went from room to room, giving food to the sick and isolated people. I remember the details of that day not only because it called up all that was the worst of divorce, but because the actual doing, the immersion in the taking the trays from the cart, walking into the rooms of people who were truly alone and fragile, trying to make conversation, attempting and sometime getting people to smile or give me toothless laughs, all of it that day, it lifted me.

"Take action: get involved" was my mother's counsel. It was not on act of selflessness. On the contrary, it became a way toward self-fullness. Through the example of my mother, volunteering became a mantra of sorts, to guide me in a path that was connected to many paths of energy and hope.

*"Volunteers are the only human beings on the face
of this earth who reflect this nation's compassion,
unselfishness, caring, patience, need, and just plain
loving one another. Their very presence transcends
politics, religion, ethnic background, martial
status, and sexism, even smokers vs. non-smokers.
It frightens me, somehow to imagine what
the world will be like without them."*

My mother not only advocated the importance of volunteering to her children, she was the volunteer advocate for the larger community, promoting its significance, and motivating others to join in her efforts. Indeed, when my mother died, the two local daily newspapers ran stories about her life with the headline "Leading Volunteer Dies."

My mother's first volunteer role was with the American Heart Association in the early 1960s where she volunteered to be a neighborhood captain and collect money from a few houses on our streets.

*"Serving an organization affords us the
opportunity to make a positive difference in
the world. These activities bring great meaning*

to our lives. Offering to volunteer also provides
free on the job training and extensive practice
in a variety of skills, from public speaking to
running a major event. But what has been
far more valuable to me has been the caliber
of people with whom I have had the
privilege of volunteering."

From this minor role, when my brother and I were children, Mom eventually joined the board of more than twenty nonprofit organizations in the area, and she spoke passionately and determinedly about the importance of volunteering and being engaged in the community around us.

I remember as a little girl watching with pride as Mom went from street captain to neighborhood captain, where she had four neighborhood blocks to organize with donations to the American Heart Association, to the chairperson of the Heart Association campaign in the entire town and then throughout northeast Pennsylvania.

Watching her, I thought Mom had a specific approach that sustained her success and her leadership in the community.

She took risks and was not afraid of more responsibility.

She was extremely organized and would follow up conscientiously before the task had to be completed. I never knew Mom to procrastinate.

She had lists, files, to-do's always on her desk, which she would cross out as soon as something was completed.

She knew how to delegate. She would figure out people's talents, give them jobs, and give everyone else credit for the success.

My mother would be heading up a huge campaign for the region—for Home Health Care, for Family Service, or the United Way—and would say to me, "I held a meeting of my committee and gave everyone a specific responsibility, and my only responsibility now is to follow up."

She praised and complimented people when they did a good job. What made Mom an effective manager was the authenticity of the praise. She gave it when people deserved it, but she praised and recognized others' contributions continually.

Volunteering for my mother was many things. First, it presented a challenge of getting things done, doing it well, and having a tangible sense of accomplishment. Then it became a way to be creative, to come up with new ideas for organizations, and then mobilize others to support her goals. Mom loved going to meetings and coming up with innovative ways for her organizations to make an impact. She would call me to say, "I had the best, most wonderful day today. I went to a board meeting, and we brainstormed so many new ideas for our next fundraising event. I cannot imagine a better day!"

"The rewards of volunteering are some of the best kept secrets. Volunteering enables you to be creative, to acquire new skills, and to push your thinking."

Mom was an idea person. She always had ideas for her organizations, for creating new ways to engage people about an issue, and for spreading her enthusiasm. Whatever she was working on, she felt passionately about the cause and would devise and develop new approaches to raise awareness—from the "End Spanking" campaign to supporting education for single mothers with children, to interfaith education, to planning strategies for children in foster care, to supporting the philharmonic orchestra and the art museums, to visiting nurses and home health services, to promoting the quality of education at Penn State, Kings College, Wilkes University, and Misericordia University, to bringing and funding an astronomy dome on Penn State campus, to strengthening the programs at Family Service, to chairing campaigns for United Way. To all these activities and issues, she would bring a mixture of positive ideas and deliberate management skills.

It was fun to brainstorm and build ideas with her. One Passover, at my home, I invited a friend Robi Damelin, to join us. Robi, an Israeli, is a member of the Parents' Circle, a group of bereaved Israelis and Palestinians who have lost loved ones in the conflict—but instead of harboring revenge, they have worked to build reconciliation through education programs for both populations.

Robi was in the United States to raise money for the organization and was telling us how difficult it was. Robi was a member of the Parents Circle because her son David had been killed the year before by a Palestinian sniper when he was serving in the Israeli reserves. Robi was still grieving and mourning her son and was a passionate advocate of peace.

At that Passover dinner, she was wearing a beautiful blue bracelet made by an Israeli artist, a woman whose brother had died in the conflict and was a member of the Parents' Circle as well. My mother complimented her bracelet, and Robi took it off her wrist and gave it to my mother.

My mother looked at the bracelet and simply said, "Why don't you call it the Peace Bracelet and raise money with it? Everyone who wears it will then make a statement that they believe in reconciliation."

The bracelet sold for more than 5 years—at every event the Parents' Circle had around the world and at every fundraising effort they conducted. Tens of thousands of dollars were raised over the two years that the "peace bracelet" was sold—and of course every single person my mother knew wore the bracelet.

> *"Not only do we need to strike a philosophical or emotional chord with people, I think we need to strike a passionate one. I know it is very important to be logical, but it is also important to feel something very deeply and passionately."*

Mom would often cite her parents when she talked about

her passion for volunteering. Mom would talk about how her parents were immigrants to this country from Russia and how they emphasized the importance of giving to the community around her. I recently found an article from the daily newspaper in Wilkes Barre reporting about my mother when she accepted an award for her volunteering efforts, it said:

Pauly Friedman is quick to downplay her own involvement but speaks freely of many other volunteers she's known, including her own parents. She said her own childhood experiences set the example for her life of service.

"Children really reflect what they see in the home. I came from a home where my parents were immigrants and so thrilled to be here in the United States that they saw volunteering as a privilege. My father was an air raid warden during World War II. He would leave the house with a flashlight and the lights would all be out. We lived in a very safe neighborhood but he was such a hero to my sisters and me. I just came naturally to think this is what you do, you give back to the community, and I passed it on to my children. Hopefully, they or I will pass it on to my grandchildren. I hope they will be instilled with the spirit of volunteering and enrich their lives."

Friedman says it is she who has benefited from the countless hours she has spent on boards and committees. "Volunteering gives meaning and purpose to your life. It makes it about something more than just thinking about yourself and being self-indulgent. The friends that you make in volunteering, the feeling of joy you get is something that you treasure throughout your life. Whatever you give, you get back ten-fold."

> *"Success is not what you have,*
> *it is what you have given away."*

Volunteering, for my mother, was about creativity, a sense of accomplishment, a management skill, a use of her talents and energy. It was also about something else. It was the understanding that making a contribution to something larger than ourselves makes us larger and continues us.

> *"Choose life which enlarges us, involves us,*
> *and continues us. In choosing this life, we discover*
> *its capacity for good is this: as we share with*
> *the others the treasures of living, we increase*
> *them for ourselves, choose to be involved,*
> *choose to live, choose life."*

Epilogue

MY MOTHER CREATED AND SUSTAINED A HAPPY, POSITIVE attitude in many ways. She enjoyed immensely what life provided her and found methods to accept with courage and humor what life denied her.

Fundamental to her way of life was her emphasis not just on pleasure but on purpose, of living not just for yourself, but for others. What surrounded her, what emanated from her, what energized her, and what remains still, is love.

And love is what propelled me to write about my mother. And as I consider it, as simple as it sounds, love is the most fundamental and powerful theme of my mother's legacy. Showing love for her family, friends, community, nature, and each day—that is the core of my mother's happiness.

So, have I learned anything? Has my behavior or attitude changed in writing this ? Have I been able to dull my negativity with the words that I have written? It took a surprising three years to write this distillation of my mother's philosophy of life.

When I explain to others why it took so long to write this, I typically say, it is because I have a demanding job and am involved (thank you, Mom) in so many volunteer activities that I did not have much time to write. But the other truth is that this writing was my priority for my summer months, when Dave, my partner, was bike riding, golfing, or reading, I would write and rewrite these passages trying to capture my mother's spirit and trying to include the details of her life that gave it meaning.

It was difficult. I would get annoyed that the writing was taking so long, or I would press myself to remember uncertain details buried in my brain that would make my mother come alive again.

But the process of unearthing these details and the prolonged time specifically spent remembering, reviewing, and rewriting became as well the process to absorb my mother's advice without any protest. My defenses to counter my mother's unyielding exuberance no longer exist.

Instead, I now find myself repeating to my children, friends, and colleagues pieces of my mother's advice that I now hold to be my own.

I have to admit, the process too has given me a different appreciation for the power of happiness. And there are times I even feel it.

About the Author

ANNE FRIEDMAN GLAUBER is a managing partner and the founder of the Global Issues practice at Finn Partners. Her work in public relations and corporate social responsibility has earned her numerous awards and national recognition for her innovative approaches to communications. In addition to her public relations work for major corporations, foundation and nonprofit organizations, she has spearheaded new ways for the private sector to address social problems.

Anne is one of the founders of NO MORE (www .nomore.org), the first national effort to unify domestic violence and sexual assault organizations across the nation under one overarching symbol. She also was the cofounder and chairperson of the Business Council for Peace (BPeace), a nonprofit organization that builds businesses for women in regions of conflict and post-conflict.

Anne's writing has appeared in *USA Today*, *The New York Times*, and *The Wall Street Journal*, among many others. She is a contributor to *Being Myself: Reflections of Growing up Female*, edited by Willa Shalit, and *Mapping the New World of American Philanthropy: Causes and Consequences of the Transfer of Wealth*, edited by Dr. Susan Raymond. Currently, she is the co-author, with Steve Klausner, of the forthcoming book *Falling into Grace* (Changing Lives Press).